Amy and Jack are on holiday.
They are visiting Max. It is dark.
Max is sleeping. But they cannot sleep!

Hamsters are nocturnal animals. They sleep in the day and they are awake at night. Children are not nocturnal!

hamster

nocturnal *sleeping in the day*

awake *not sleeping*

Tonight the children are camping. Suddenly, Amy points. 'Look!' She says. 'What are they? Are they birds?'

cave

No, they are bats. Bats are nocturnal. They sleep in caves in the day. At night they find food.

Bats eat insects. How do they catch insects in the dark? Bats have got weak eyes, but they hear well.

bat

The children are not scared of the dark. Max has got a torch. Suddenly, Max jumps. 'What's that?'

It has got big eyes and big wings. It is a bird.
A nocturnal bird. What is it?

torch

It is an owl! The children are not scared.
Mice are scared. Owls eat mice! Owls and mice
are nocturnal.

owl

Owls have got big eyes. They can see well in the dark. Owls fly very quietly. Mice cannot hear them.

Today it is Max's birthday. Look at the candles on his cake. Look at all the moths! The children laugh.

Moths are usually nocturnal. Butterflies are not nocturnal. Moths sleep with their wings open. Butterflies sleep with their wings closed.

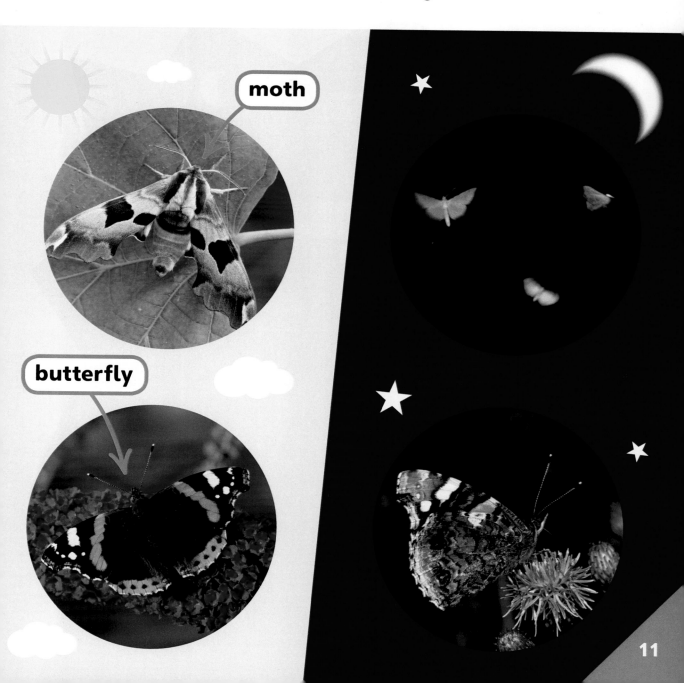

moth

butterfly

Suddenly, the family hears a loud noise.
It is the chickens! Uncle Jim is angry.
'What is it?' Max asks.

It is a fox! Foxes are nocturnal.
They eat chickens with their sharp teeth.
But the chickens are safe tonight.

Home again! Amy and Jack are very tired, but they are happy. There are no nocturnal animals at home!
'Goodnight!'

Before You Read

1 Match the words and pictures.

owl   hamster   mouse   bat   moth   fox

After You Read

1 Read and answer Yes (Y) or No (N).

- [ ] Do nocturnal animals sleep in the day?
- [ ] Do bats have good eyes?
- [ ] Are butterflies nocturnal?
- [ ] Do foxes eat chickens?

2 Look at page 14. What nocturnal animals can you see?

Pearson Education Limited
Edinburgh Gate, Harlow,
Essex CM20 2JE, England
and Associated Companies throughout the world.

ISBN: 978-1-4082-8828-3

This edition first published by Pearson Education Ltd 2013
13
Text copyright © Pearson Education Ltd 2013

The moral rights of the author have been asserted
in accordance with the Copyright Designs and Patents Act 1988

Set in 19/23pt OT Fiendstar
Printed in China
SWTC/13

Acknowledgements
The publisher would like to thank the following for their kind permission to reproduce their photographs:
(Key: b-bottom; c-centre; l-left; r-right; t-top)

Alamy Images: imagebroker 4, Papilio 2b; **Ardea**: John Daniels 13, Jean Michel Labat 9t, Adrian Warren 11tr;
FLPA Images of Nature: Chris Brignell 8, Franz Christoph Robi / Imagebroker 5, ImageBroker 11br; **Fotolia.com**:
Eric Isselee 15tr; **Nature Picture Library**: Stephan Dalton 11bl, Andy Sands 11tl; **Rex Features**: Nigel Barklie 2t;
Shutterstock.com: Alexander Ischenko 15cr, Alexander Ishchenko 9b, Chas 15br, Eric Isselee 15tl, 15bl,
Kirsanov 15cl)
Cover images: *Front*: **Shutterstock.com**: Mark Bridger; *Back*: **Shutterstock.com**: Kirsanov

All other images © Pearson Education

In some instances we have been unable to trace the owners of copyright material,
and we would appreciate any information that would enable us to do so.

Illustrations: Andrew Roland (Advocate)

For a complete list of the titles available in the Pearson English Kids Readers series, please go to
www.pearsonenglishkidsreaders.com. Alternatively, write to your local Pearson Education office or to
Pearson English Readers Marketing Department, Pearson Education, Edinburgh Gate, Harlow, Essex CM202JE, England.